25 Days *of*
Holiday Organizing

25 Days of Holiday Organizing

by Jul's Arthur

25 Days of Holiday Organizing
Copyright © 2020 by Jul's Arthur
Published by Royal Essex Publishing
Production Director: Janet Spencer King, www.spencerkingauthorservices.com
Cover/Interior Design: Steven Plummer, www.spbookdesign.com
Photos of Jul's: Christa Meola, www.christameola.com

Printed in the United States of American for Worldwide Distribution

ISBN: 978-1-7334474-0-9

To my sons, Tyryn Whitney and Skylyr Winslow.
You are, and always will be, my daily blessing, lighting up my life and very existence. You give meaning to the word LOVE! Because of you two boys, holidays were always brilliant fun!

To my mother, Mery, who truly believes in my every endeavor.

To my clients who honored me with the opportunity to take them from *chaos* to CLARITY.

Table of Contents

Welcome!

I'M SO THRILLED to connect with you!

I'm Jul's, your new personal organizer.

(That's not a typo in my name, by the way. There's a story behind that apostrophe. And that story is for another day.)

In case you don't know me already, I help people simplify their spaces and lives with customized easy systems so they can feel happier, get more enjoyment out of life and be less stressed.

When most people meet a professional organizer, immediately they'll say, "Oh your home must be so tidy. Have you always been one of those naturally super organized Type A people?"

Ahhhh ... no. Quite the opposite!

I was not born organized.

Having an older sister with that "gene" taught me that organizing did not come naturally to me. I've spent years perfecting and adjusting, making mistakes and problem-solving so that other naturally disorganized people can organize more easily.

And here's what's so amazing about my not being innately organized and so not a Type A personality ...

I get it and I get you.

I understand why you feel so overwhelmed. I understand why you feel as un-Martha-Stewart-like as can be. (Just so you know ... Martha had a whole team of people to help her do what she did.)

I understand that your kitchen table is a catch-all for everyone's stuff, your dining room table piled with papers to the point you can't remember the last time you ate there.

I've been there myself.

And since running my business, I've also worked with hundreds of women (and some men) who have told me that they were there, too. They'd given up. They just could not ever get organized. I've helped those women and men to conquer the clutter—*finally!*—and simplify in a way that made sense for them.

The holidays are a tricky time for all of us. Everyone— including me—feels ten times more overwhelmed than normal during the holidays.

That's why I've created this short yet impactful wee book—*25 Days of Holiday Organizing*—to make your holidays go more smoothly.

Although this book is geared towards Christmas in the examples, because that's the holiday we celebrate in our home, keep in mind that you can adapt these tips and organizing concepts for any holiday, and even apply them to your everyday life.

Some of the daily organizing tips may seem simple, even basic, and that is intentional. Over the past 14+ years as a professional organizer, I've found it's the little things that set us up for success.

Now that we're introduced, let me say I'm super excited you're joining me for the next *25 Days of Holiday Organizing* ...

I hope you find it a wonderful, fun gift of sanity making your holidays less chaos-filled, and more joyous and peaceful.

Together we're going to whisk away the holiday stress with my Simple Organizing Solutions (SOS) for your holidays.

When I was a child, I loved our Advent calendar. It was a daily surprise and fun countdown to Christmas opening each window and finding something special. I carried this tradition on with my own two wee boys Tyryn Whitney and Skylyr Winslow with their own Advent calendars for daily excitement. Those were a 25-day-long extravaganza!

Yet my philosophy is **less is more**. That's why I'm offering a simpler format in these *25 Days of Holiday Organizing* so you can do more with less.

The goal as always is to **actually implement** these holiday organizing tips. Each of the 25 days has one tip to tackle per day, plus real-life photo examples and helpful product links.

So, get ready to get started and Happy Christmas, Hanukkah, Kwanzaa, Ramadan and Merry Holidays to all!

Jul's xox

My sons and me: Skylyr Winslow, me (Mama) & Tyryn Whitney

(Left photo) Skylyr Winslow on my lap, me & Tyryn Whitney.
(Center top photo) Loving brothers: Ty-Ty & Skye.
(Center bottom photo) Skye's favorite place—high up a tree!

Before You Begin

To GET THE most out of this book, use it like an Advent calendar—"opening" or reading and implementing only one daily tip at a time. To avoid feeling overwhelmed, I want to caution you against skipping ahead. Focus, absorb, adapt and implement each day's tip to work for you.

Who Am I to Help Organize Your Holidays?

You might be wondering who am I to help you get organized in time for Christmas or whatever holidays you celebrate.

Well, even though I'm a professional organizer in my business, I am also a huge holidays lover!

You'll likely realize in the first few days of this book that I do not practice minimalism when it comes to Christmas decorations. It's the one area I am *not* a minimalist. At some point, when it's time to downsize, I will pare down the decorations and give my children their Christmas ornaments for their homes. (I'm sure that will be another book in itself!)

Less is more ... except at Christmas. That's when I allow myself to let loose. We do have such special decorations! Here's the backstory:

I'm not a huge collector of anything except Santas and certain Christmas ornaments. When we first moved into our house, there was a period of five or more years of my then-husband's major "renovations" that created chaos.

As extended family visited us during holiday time, I wanted to distract their focus from missing mouldings, broken plaster, gutted spaces, visible Tyvek® and destruction (oops, I mean *construction*), so I started decorating every room to cover the mess.

Back then, I did not realize that this would start a tradition of decorating our whole house for Christmas! Our home does look especially beautiful during the holidays.

Organizing Concepts

Not only will I show you exactly what to do every day for your holiday organizing, but each day you will learn and apply an organizing concept that you can then use in your life.

Here is an overview of the organizing concepts as a handy quick reference guide:

Repurposing

Think Vertical

Simplify & Clarify

Prepare Ahead

A Home For Everything

Organize Creatively

Organize For Kids

Use Quality Supplies

What To Keep

Repurposing

Repurposing is in my DNA as much as being a Type A organizer is not. I don't see things for what they are; I see them for what I want them to be.

The manufacturer intended a box as a stationery card holder; I see it as a perfect box for my hair clips and ties. The store sold me a plastic butter dish cover; it's upside down in my kitchen drawer as a perfect fit for housing my silicone garlic peeler tube.*

Repurposing allows you to create containers and systems that please you aesthetically and functionally.

 http://bit.ly/SiliconeGarlicPeeler   (*a must-have gadget)

Type the above link in your browser or you can find specific information by searching Silicone Garlic Peeler Tube on your online browser.

Think Vertical

This is one of my favorite organizing concepts. We have a house, typical of its era, that has few closets. People had a lot less stuff back then. Think pre-Amazon.

Hanging items as often as you can helps you keep things visible yet out of the way. This idea came to me from the way stores hang much of their stock and packaged items.

Hang scissors, funnels, nail clippers, wreaths and more. I love to figure out how to hang something to get it off the floor or shelf and make more room for daily-use items.

Use nails or hooks, (adhesive hooks, cup hooks, L hooks) or whatever makes best sense in an area.

Simplify & Clarify

Coming up with a theme helps to simplify and clarify what you will create or buy.

This idea started from my boys' at-home birthday parties to make them fun and memorable when the "in thing" back then was hosting kids' parties at a posh party center. I used my boys' latest passions and interests, and it was easy to find ready-made party plates, napkins, and tablecloths to create unique decorations. The boys still remember all the detailed creations I made for those theme parties.

Using themes for the holidays helps with decorations and keeps your creative mind focused.

Prepare Ahead

Preparing ahead is a life-saver when you're a single mama like me and have too much on your plate. I know you have a lot on your plate too! By thinking and planning ahead, I can find the best sales (save money), go at a leisurely pace (less stress), and still save time when the activity gets started. I'm all ready to go.

The reason many of us struggle with advance planning is we get overwhelmed with the detail of it or worry we will spend all our energy planning and not actually take action.

To make preparing ahead work for you, keep it simple. Create a list or brainstorm for a few minutes. That's it! That's all you need do. Lists help you get things done, no perfection needed. Be fluid, flexible and keep your planning light.

A Home For Everything

You know what's odd? We like to own stuff, yet so often we don't honor what we keep. When I help clients to declutter, they start to focus on what they keep not what they don't want. It's important to honor what we have.

A simple way to do this is to create a home for our items. "A place for everything and everything in its place."

Now, this is not as terrifying as it sounds. Take it one item at a time. Create homes that are convenient and near where you use the item, if possible.

I have a holiday wreath for the front door, which I love and is easy to put up, creating an instantly decorated front door. The wreath was not inexpensive when I bought it, so I protect it all year long with a dry-cleaning bag hanging over the wreath like a shirt hanger. I then hang it on a nail in the under-the-stairs closet, high up off the floor so there's more storage space below. The wreath's **home** is under the stairs hung high on a specific nail.

When creating homes for items, consider:

- Store closest to where you use
- Store where it makes sense to you (not necessarily by room)
- Stack no more than three items when nesting, unless they easily fit into each other, such as bowls, plates, etc.

Organize Creatively

When you tap into your organizing style, **take the quiz** at this address, **https://julsarthur.com/your-organization-style** —you'll be excited to find unique and inspiring ways to organize your holiday decorations and treasures.

Christmas cards are still so special to us, because though an e-card can be digitally stylized and cool, the actual cards themselves are festive while adding to holiday decor and spirit. Use your creative side to enjoy and display holiday treasures in a way that adds to your and your family's pleasure.

Organize For Kids

I love what organizing can do to make our lives better and our families happier. When you organize your holidays to make them kid-friendly, you avoid the fighting and worries that can add to holiday stress.

What traditions can you create to keep your holidays special? What is the simplest way to establish those traditions and keep them easy to repeat?

Keep your kids in mind when you organize if they are going to need to reach or retrieve items. Store at their level and contain in portable ways so they can gather supplies and put them back easily.

Use Quality Supplies

Our first Christmas tree stand defied the laws of gravity ... and lost. We would have been better off with a bucket of rocks and sand! We were in the kitchen drinking hot cocoa, when all of a sudden: **Crash!** It was a big tree and we lost several ornaments when it fell over. The replacement stand we bought is super heavy and does the job no matter how big the tree. Lesson learned.

It was a lesson learned the hard way. I was in tears over broken special glass ornaments from Europe. Every year now, I bless our heavy cast iron tree stand. Well-made organizing supplies are oh-so-worth it!

What To Keep

If there was one key organizing concept that applies to everything, it could be summed up in what I tell my decluttering clients:

"You can keep whatever you want, as long as it doesn't keep you."

The key is to honor what you choose to hold onto and keep it special by displaying it and then putting it away, storing cleverly to keep the lasting joy for years to come.

READY TO GET STARTED?

ONWARDS TO DAY 1!
Singing "The 12 Days of Christmas" as you go ...

"On the first day of Christmas my personal organizer sent to me, this Simply Organized tip!"

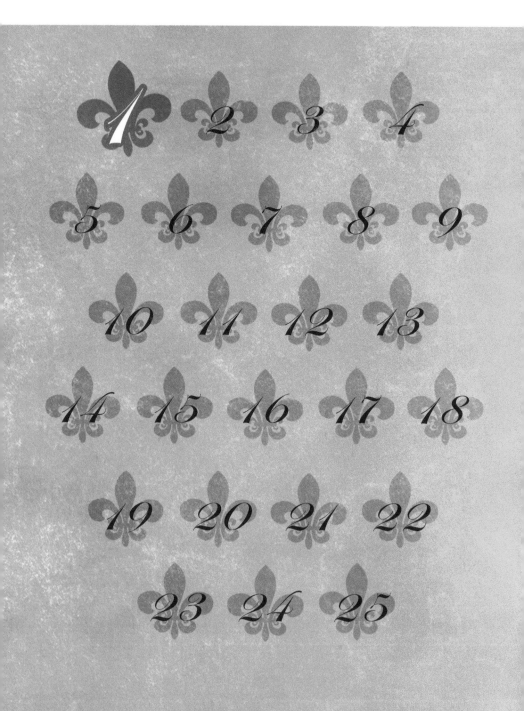

TIP: Repurpose a food or fruit gift box for fragile ornament storage.

ID YOU RECEIVE any food or fruit gift boxes this holiday season? Hold onto them so that you can repurpose!

These boxes are ideal for storing fragile ornaments after the holidays are over. The dividers in these gift boxes often have crinkle paper in them, which keeps your breakable ornaments safe.

The photo of the first box was a pear and cheese gift box and came with tissue paper, so we reused the paper to wrap our collection of Christmas snow globes, storing them in this box.

The second box was a fruit gift box filled with fresh apples and pears nestled in crinkle paper. We repurposed the box to store our fragile Christmas tree ornaments in it.

A lovely gift box of pears and cheese
now stores fragile ornaments.

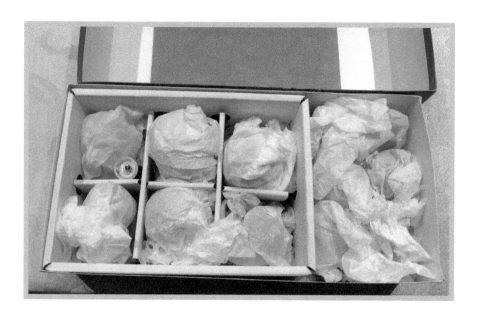

A sturdy holiday gift fruit box keeps our delicate ornaments safe all year.

A cheese and fruit box
from a corporate client
stores ornaments
and doubles as
part of our fireplace
decor at Christmas.

A local client loves how I repurpose airtight glass canning jars. I use the jars to keep clay ornaments safe. This repurposing idea came about because one year I discovered, with sunken heart, that mice had chewed and destroyed a precious clay ornament stored in a cardboard box. My client was so thrilled with the idea she repurposed jars for storing everyday items.

Day 1 Organizing Concept

Repurposing

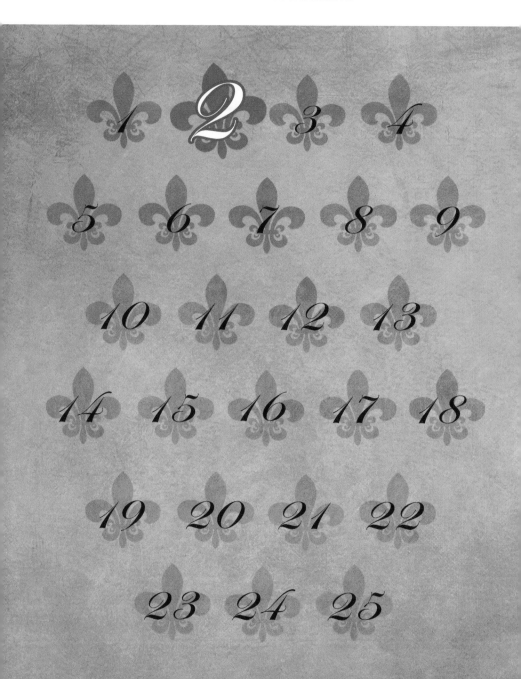

Day 2

TIP: Use under the stairs for holiday storage.

WE STORE ALL of our Christmas items under the foyer stairs. That's more impressive than you might think. Christmas is huge in our family and we have ten 18-gallon totes and several hanging items, plus the boys' mini Christmas trees to store. Honestly, I ought to give holiday storage tours with how precision-packed our "Harry Potter" closet is!

Let's get started!

Decide on a space to store your Christmas items where you can put up nails or hooks to maximize storage space. If you use under the stairs storage you will store your decorations throughout the year out of sight.

Under the foyer stairs, we make the most of the space by thinking vertically. Here's how all our Christmas decorations are stored.

Hidden "Harry Potter Christmas Closet," under the stairs, chock full of organized Christmas decoration goodies!

Stacked storage containers: totes for keeping decorations.

 http://bit.ly/18GallonLatchingStorage

Type the above link in your browser or you can find specific information by searching 18 Gallon Storage Latching Tote on your online browser.

Use nails to hang decorations on walls, to hang behind and above boxes or totes.

I love using our storage under the stairs because it's such a great use of space that doesn't impact the rest of the house. Plus it keeps all holiday items contained.

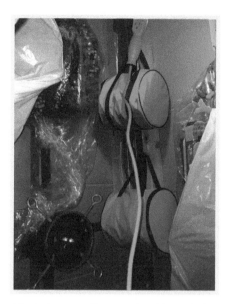

Hanging on the under-the-stairs wall are wreaths, Christmas tree lights and cast iron stand.

Bags hung under the stairs hold electronic stuffed Christmas animals and much more.

🔍 http://bit.ly/KissingBallBBB

Type the above link in your browser or you can find specific information by searching Christmas Kissing Balls on your online browser.

Hanging by their ribbons on stair tread backs, covered in tall kitchen trash bags for protection, are two artificial kissing balls.

Close-up of our heavy cast iron tree stand
hanging from a strong, long nail.

All Christmas decorations are boxed, stacked,
hung and stored under our stairs.

BONUS *Tip*

Decorate early so everyone can enjoy the festive season for many weeks. Set up your holiday decorations just after Thanksgiving.

Storage doesn't have to be picture perfect! Vertical storage helps fit more items safely organized out of the way.

Day 2 Organizing Concept

Think Vertical

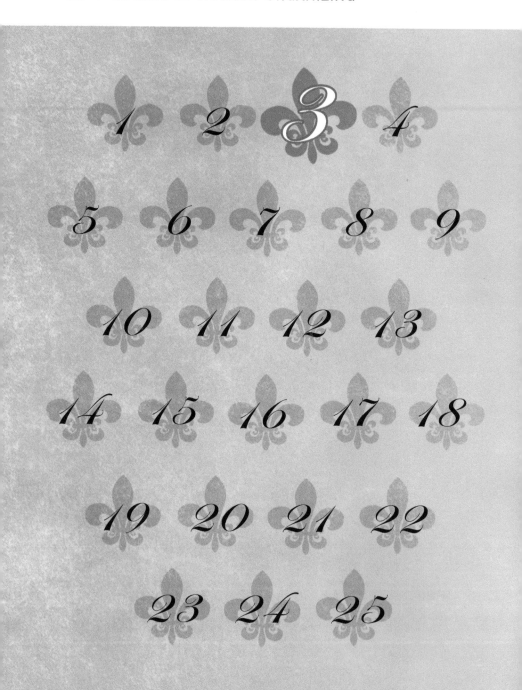

Day 3

TIP: Maximize wreath storage.

I CAN'T EMPHASIZE THIS enough for storage— **think vertical!** It's one of the best organizing tips you can learn and I apply it whenever I can. Vertical storage is easy, out of the way, and maximizes an otherwise small space such as under the stairs. Just hammer in an appropriate nail on the back of a stair tread or on the walls. Voilà.

I've helped my customers to hang all their holiday wreaths on closet walls, garage walls and under the stairs. They always say how simple it is, but also so effective.

I repurpose dry-cleaning wire hangers and the clear plastic covers that come with them to store artificial wreaths and other decorations. You can also use kitchen trash bags.

Poke the hanger through the bottom of the bag, which will now become the top of the bag over your item. The plastic bags protect wreaths and decorations from dust.

Clear plastic dry-cleaner bag repurposed to store our front door Christmas wreath. We store this wreath by hanging it on the wall under the stairs as shown on Day 2.

Back of wreath:
Hanging decorative
wreaths.

Client basement
storage where I hung
all her wreaths.

I love hanging wreaths vertically because then they're ready to
go when decoration time arrives.

Note

Take care with plastic bags around children. When the boys were wee ones, I was careful not to keep the plastic dry-cleaning bags anywhere near them for safety. However, if you can, it's great to be able to repurpose the plastic and not have to throw it in the trash.

A funny tale from a client experience:

The husband of one of my clients, in the 1980s, insisted on having a bomb shelter room built in their basement. She always thought he was being a bit over the top, though she kept her humor. The odd-shaped room never got used at all. When I helped her organize, I hammered in nails on the shelter walls and hung all her holiday wreaths. She was tickled pink that finally this room had purpose and brought happiness every time she opened the door to retrieve a holiday wreath.

Day 3 Organizing Concept

Think Vertical

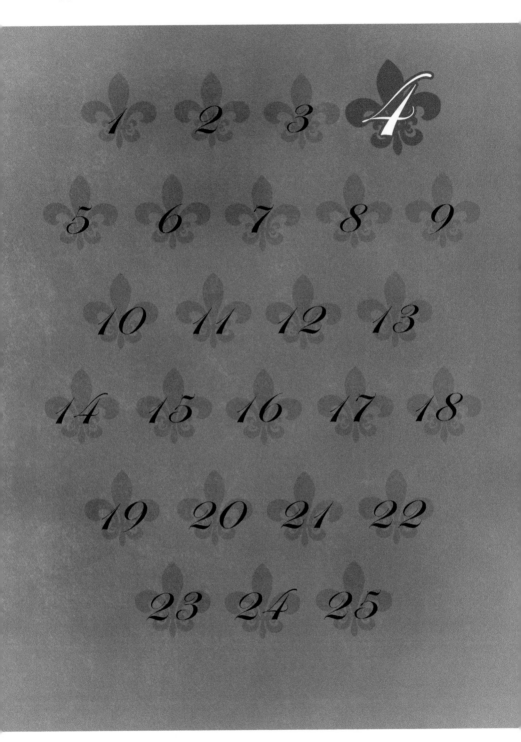

Day 4

TIP: For gift-giving made simple, think theme.

ECIDING ON A theme for gifts and then finding those items on sale means you're rockin' it!

One year, I chose scarves and gloves as a theme. It made gift-giving so easy, as I bought lovely gloves and scarves for my sisters, nieces, and girlfriends. Getting them on sale meant I could give more and better gifts. (I found such great scarves I even bought a couple for myself and still wear them daily to ward off the New England cold from October through March.)

When you decide on a theme, it focuses your mind to come up with quick ideas. And while shopping, it puts a pause on impulse buying.

Items also often come in alternative colors, which makes gift-purchasing even easier. Say you choose cashmere scarves. It's so simple to give everyone a color suited to them, so the gifts look different enough, but for you, they were easy to find all together.

Here's some gift themes:

- ❖ Jewelry
- ❖ Travel accessories
- ❖ Board games
- ❖ Magazine subscriptions
- ❖ Scarves
- ❖ Food
- ❖ Personalized stationery
- ❖ Gift cards
- ❖ Books
- ❖ Tickets for movies and shows
- ❖ Gloves
- ❖ Bath products

And here's what happens when you make a theme. You find them all in one place.

Scarves are wonderful accessories!

Scarf ideas for lasses:

Lasses' Scarves

 http://bit.ly/ScarvesWomen

Faux Fur Wrap

 http://bit.ly/FauxFurWrap

Type the above links in your browser or you can find specific information for Women's Scarves and Women's Faux Fur Wraps on your online browser.

Scarves work well as gifts for men.

Scarf ideas for lads:

Scarves for Men

 http://bit.ly/GapMenScarves

Lads' Scarves

 http://bit.ly/LadsScarves

Type the above links in your browser or you can find specific information for Men's Scarves on your online browser.

Glove ideas for friends:

Gloves for Women

🔍 http://bit.ly/CheetahGloves

Gloves for Men

🔍 http://bit.ly/GlovesForMen

Type the above links in your browser or you can find specific information for Women's Gloves and Men's Gloves on your online browser.

Love gloves and mittens. Practical and who doesn't need a new pair due to a lost mate?

JUST FOR *Fun*

Check out this awesome video on YouTube.com, 25 Ways to Wear a Scarf in 4.5 Minutes—http://bit.ly/WendyNguyen25WaysScarf by Wendy Nguyen of Wendy's Lookbook—http://www.wendyslookbook.com/.

An event planner friend told me she loved my use of theme thinking. I helped her with creating a holiday event, "A Night In Paris", at the Museum of Natural History in Manhattan. There was a painted backdrop of the Eiffel Tower, a French couture fashion show, and catered French holiday food.

Day 4 Organizing Concept

Simplify & Clarify

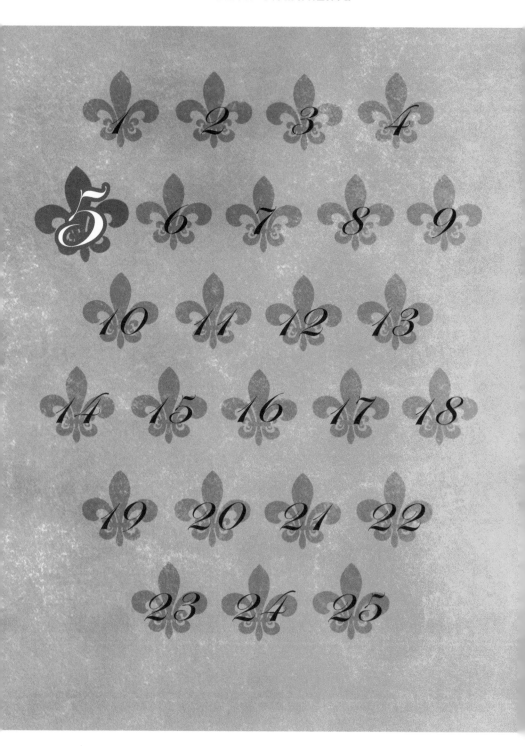

Day 5

TIP: Make gift-giving easy—save time & money.

O N DAY 4, I let you in on the decision-saving secret of themed gift-giving. Want to go all out and make next year's holiday easy on your time and wallet? Holiday shop in January a year ahead.

Now I understand ... it's easy to feel shopped-out and the crowds can be a drag. But if you focus on how easy the holiday will be next year, you'll move forward with energy.

Let's say you've decided your gift-giving theme is a long-sleeve shirt for everyone. You shop the January sales and maybe that means your budget allows for some designer purchases.

Write a list of everyone you need to buy gifts. Once you purchase gifts, wrap and label them.

This next tip is so important. Take a Post-it® note, and write a description of the gift so you recall what it is a year later. You can also snap a photo of the gift and tape it to the back of the wrapped gift. Be sure to include the gift recipient's name.

One year my gift theme was warm, button-down shirts.

One of my clients left me a voicemail after we organized her entire house. She began by telling me she was calling from hospital as she had an unexpected health scare. Her voice was surprisingly calm. She reported the one thing that was keeping her positive and coping so well was the thought that her home was now totally organized and she had no worries about preparing for the holidays.

Day 5 Organizing Concept

Prepare Ahead

Day 6

TIP: Get your gift bag storage sorted.

*H*AVING YOUR GIFT-WRAPPING accessories organized makes holiday time so much easier. And today's tip is going to make that happen.

Mise en place, as the French say, meaning everything has a set place.

Just like when you're cooking, setting up your kitchen utensils and tools within easy reach makes the task go smoothly.

You'll notice in my photo of my Gift Bag Organizer, I don't fuss and make the bags all perfect. I'm like you—busy! I just fold and put my bags in the holder. So though it may not look like a magazine perfect photo ... it's real and the bags work well for holding and presenting gifts.

I love using holiday gift bags because wrapping gifts is as simple as putting in a couple sheets of tissue paper, the gift, a gift label and you're done. You can always add ribbons and bows if you want.

The bags are reusable and I tie my gift labels on the handle of the bags rather than stick or tape them on, so the recipient is able to reuse the gift bag.

Create your own gift bag organizer and hang it in a closet near where you wrap gifts. The purpose is to store and keep gift bags organized for easy retrieval without taking up too much space.

Here is a link for purchasing a Gift Bag Organizer as well as a photo example of my own.

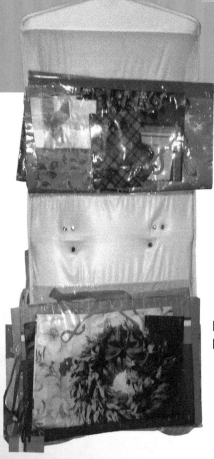

Gift Bag Organizer

🔍 http://bit.ly/GiftBagOrganizer

Type the above link in your browser or you can find specific information by searching Gift Bag Organizer on your online browser.

Hanging Gift
Bag Organizer.

Day 6 Organizing Concept

A Home for Everything

Day 7

TIP: Set up your Wrap Zone.

WHEN YOU SET up a wrap zone, you make it easier, quicker and more inspiring to wrap gifts.

First, get yourself a good Gift Wrap Organizer. There are a few different ones, so I've added some links below, as well as a photo of mine.

The beauty of these organizers is they store all the wrapping accessories in one place. I choose to have one Gift **Bag** Organizer and one Gift **Wrap** Organizer, simply because I use a lot of gift bags. You can find them in craft stores or online.

Mine holds:

- Scotch Tape
- scissors
- gift tags
- ribbons
- bows

You can divide the gift wrap organizer so that you use one side for Christmas or holiday wrap, and one for all occasion, birthday, wedding, baby etc.

Here's where you can get yours:

Gift Wrap Organizer

🔍 https://bit.ly/Wrap-Organizer

Wrapping Organizer

🔍 http://bit.ly/WrapOrganizer

Type the above links in your browser or you can find specific information by searching Gift Bag Organizer and Wrapping Paper Organizer on your online browser.

Hanging Gift Wrap Organizer: Rolls, bows, scissors, tape, and more.

I prefer a hanging gift wrap organizer, but if you prefer under the bed, you can find them as well.

As someone who was not born organized, simplicity is something I strive for daily to invite more calm and happiness into my life.

And that's my strength as an organizing coach. Bringing calm to my clients, sometimes for the first time.

Stick with your Advent organizing, because this work is life-changing. I know that because I get it! And my clients find it so as well.

Especially if you're a creative type and have a brain that works fast like me and many of my clients, getting organized will be about progress, not perfection. You've finished the first week, so keep focused and keep going!

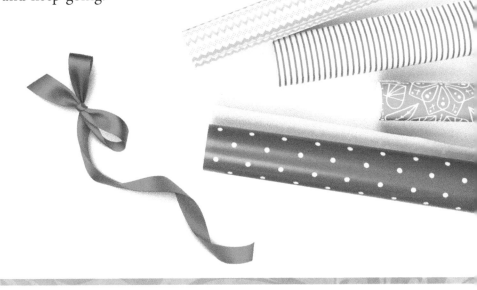

Day 7 Organizing Concept

A Home for Everything

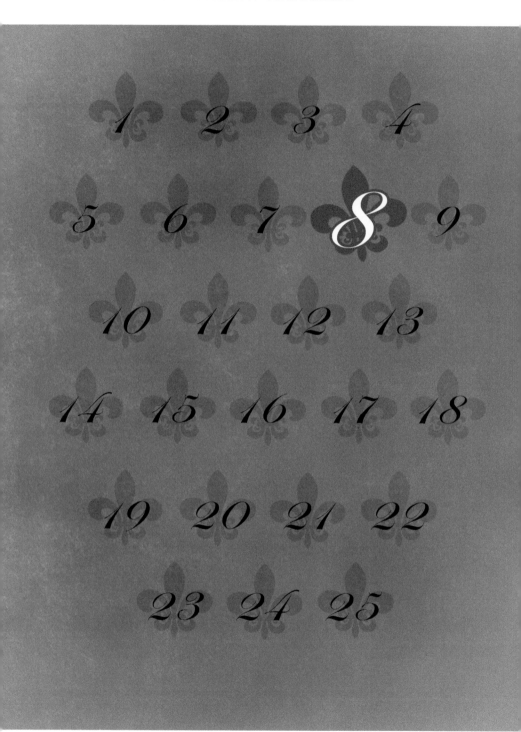

Day 8

TIP: Organize your holiday-light storage.

I USE DUFFEL BAGS for storing our Christmas lights. Each bag comes with four plastic reels that holds two sets of up to 100 lights each.

The handles make these zipper bags easy to use and I hang each bag from a nail under our foyer stairs.

Here's the insider knowledge you need to know: Write or type up tips for stringing your lights and store them with your lights! This will save you each year when you've forgotten which end of the light to start with first and for best steps.

Stringing lights is a messy job. I know because I am the resident family Christmas-Tree Light Stringer by default. It saves me so much time to refer to the tips I've learned along the way by having them front and center when I unpack the lights, instead of trying to remember what I did last year.

I string 1,000 mini lights on our tree. That's a lot of lights! Every little time-saving tip is key.

Holiday lights wrapped on reels, stored in duffle
bags with typed tips for efficient lighting.

It took a few Christmases for me to find a way to store lights that worked for me and keep the lights in working order.

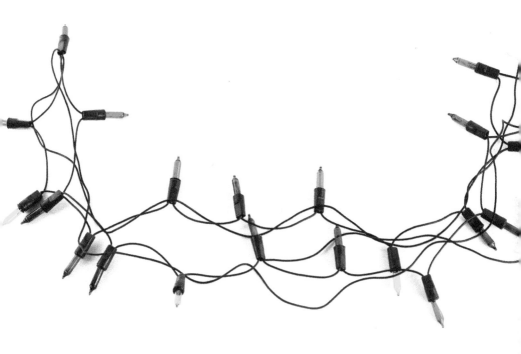

Day 8 Organizing Concept

A Home for Everything

Day 9

TIP: Holiday card organizing 101.

IN OUR FAMILY, we organize and display our cards so that we can enjoy them, hanging them on a ribbon.

Supplies:

- ⚜ Ribbon about 1/4" wide; color of choice
- ⚜ Mini clothespins; color of choice
- ⚜ Holiday cards from family and friends

Step 1:

String a ribbon between two points. (In our dining room, we use a Christmas red ribbon tied to handle pulls between two of our built-in china cabinets.) Handles on an unused fireplace screen, cabinets or two hooks will also work just fine.

Hanging holiday cards so everyone can enjoy them.

Step 2:

As each card comes in, use a mini clothespin on the top corner of the card to hang it on the ribbon. We use mini Christmas green and red clothespins.

Thin red ribbon and
Christmas-colored mini clothespins.

Ribbon tied to handle
pulls between cabinets.

It's easy to add cards to the ribbon as they arrive in the mail.

Day 9 Organizing Concept

Organize Creatively

Day 10

TIP: Display your holiday cards another way.

*I*F YOU GET lots of cards, such as my client who receives over 200 cards each Christmas, this method is an easy DIY solution.

Supplies:

- ⚜ Yarn; color of choice
- ⚜ Pringles® potato chip container with lid or one with similar shape and size
- ⚜ Holiday cards from family and friends

String the yarn through one end of the container and knot it.

Step 1:

Keep the lid and empty Pringles® container.

Step 2:

Use a can opener and remove the bottom so the container now is open on both ends.

Step 3:

String the yarn through one end of the container and knot it so you can keep winding end to end. The yarn is to cover the container each strand next to the other and tangle-free.

Step 4:

Once the yarn strands fully cover the container, cut and knot the end to tie off.

Step 5:

Put the plastic lid on. You can cover the lid in aluminum foil to hide the plastic. You can also stick a ribbon on top.

Keep stringing the yarn end to end to cover the can.

Cover the lid with foil and stick a ribbon on top.

Step 6:

Open each holiday card and slide it through a single strand of yarn so the cards create a fan.

Open each card; slide it through a single strand of yarn.

Once you make this card holder, it can be used over and over. One of my clients receives over 400 cards each Christmas—I had to make her two of these Pringles® card holders to organize her cards.

Holiday Card Fan; display and store hundreds of cards.

Day 10 Organizing Concept

Organize Creatively

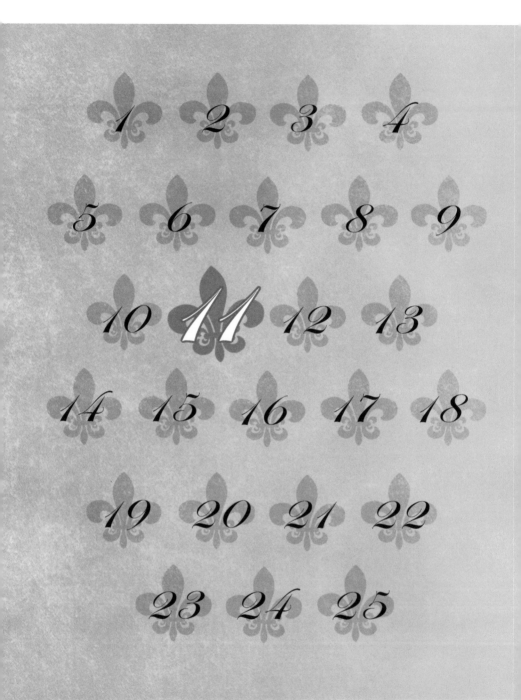

Day 11

TIP: Take kid-friendly decorating to a new level.

ONE OF THE best things I did for my young sons was involve them in holiday decorating.

I brought to my marriage many fragile and handmade glass ornaments from England and other European treasures. Once my children arrived, it became apparent the Christmas tree would have to be rethought. I didn't want my sons' childhood Christmas memories to be their mama saying "No!" all the time as they tried to reach for fragile ornaments.

It seemed simple to just put non-breakables on the lower branches, so I did that. However, I decided to get a small artificial tree for my first-born son for him to decorate. It was such a success that we repeated the exercise for his baby brother later on.

The boys loved having their own decorations and their own lighted tree. They would busily decorate their trees with non-breakable ornaments and needed no redirecting from our big tree. It was such a delight not to be telling the boys, "No, don't touch that!" because they were so proud of their own trees.

Ty-Ty's and Skye's trees are part of our family tradition now. Give it a try. Have a baby artificial tree with non-breakable ornaments for your children to divert attention from the more delicate decorations.

Skylyr's Christmas Tree

SECRET *Tip*

Now my sons are older and no longer enjoy decorating the trees, I store them fully decorated, lights and all. However, for years, the boys loved getting their box of stored ornaments and decorating the tree with every ornament on one branch!

Tyryn's
Christmas Tree

Plastic dry-cleaning bag to protect
artificial tree during storage.

BONUS *Tip*

I reuse a plastic bag from the dry cleaners to cover the tree while storing it. It keeps the tree dust-free and preserved.

Every year, one of my clients helps keep her kids organized with this holiday tradition. Her kids each donate a gently used toy or game to a local shelter. She says her children have learned the value of helping others with this simple tradition.

DAY 11: Organizing Concept

Organize for Kids

Day 12

TIP: Get a super sturdy Christmas tree stand!

OUR MOVE FROM Manhattan to Connecticut gave us a house for the first time instead of an apartment. There were also local tree farms nearby to get big fresh Christmas trees to fit our 8-foot ceilings. As I noted earlier, my naiveté about setting up the Christmas tree had disastrous results.

That first year, we went to WalMart and bought a Christmas tree stand. Once the tree was all decorated, lights and ornaments looking so beautiful, we happily went to the kitchen for cocoa. And then **crash!**

I can't recall how many broken ornaments I cried over that evening, but it was enough to spur me to action.

Having learned my lesson, I was willing to spend a good $60 on a cast iron—majorly sturdy, very heavy, the real deal—Christmas tree stand. And may I say, we've never had our tree fall again.

Don't skimp on the tree stand. Trust me! Get one that is durable and sturdy.

Cast iron super sturdy tree stand; never had a tree mishap since!

Tree stand stored hanging on
the under-the-stairs wall.

Day 12 Organizing Concept

Use Quality Supplies

TIP: Buy a green power strip protector.

THIS IS MY #1 Christmas Tree Lighting Pro Tip.
If you string a lot of lights on your Christmas tree, like I do, to stay safe connect only the amount of light sets that your set-up can handle. The package with your strings of lights will tell you how many sets you can safely connect per outlet.

Fortunately, you can use a power strip, which will add extra outlets to the traditional two in wall sockets. Having a green strip camouflages well with the tree. An additional plus is the power strip has an on/off toggle so it's easy to turn the lights on and off without messing up the tree. Search your internet browser for green power strips.

Dark green power buttoned strip for easy Christmas tree lighting.

Day 13 Organizing Concept

Use Quality Supplies

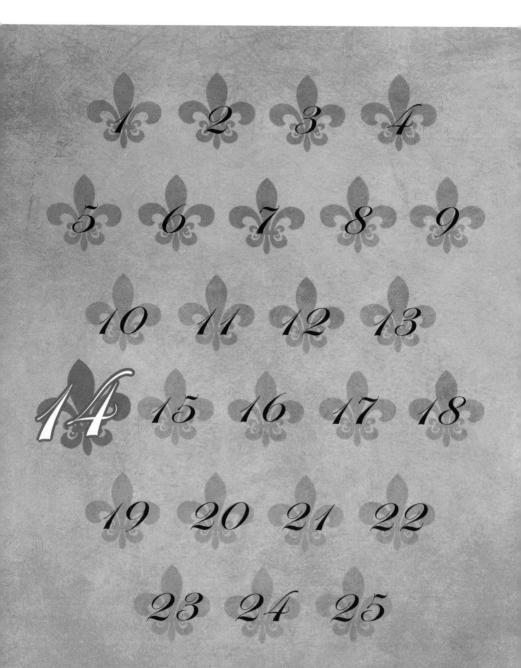

Day 14

TIP: Check your light strands before stringing them on the tree!

THERE'S NOTHING WORSE than having strung an entire light string and discovering that half the lights no longer light up. We used to spend time finding which bulb in the strand was not working and go through my collection of extra bulbs to replace the dead one. The worst was when a light strand would not light up at all and we would take a bulb tester and tediously test each bulb to find the bad one.

Christmas Tree Lighting Pro Tip #2!

Finally, I came up with a better solution. Each year, I go to the store after Christmas when the light sets are 50% off. I buy several 100-bulb mini multi-color light sets for the tree and a couple of 100-bulb clear light sets for the outside lighting on our front porch garland. I store these for the next Christmas.

If a set we've stored has somehow gone bad—and mysteriously at least one set does every year, even though it worked when we stored it—I simply replace it with one of our new sets.

Sometimes saving time and keeping it simple is the way to go.

DAY 14: Organizing Concept

Prepare Ahead

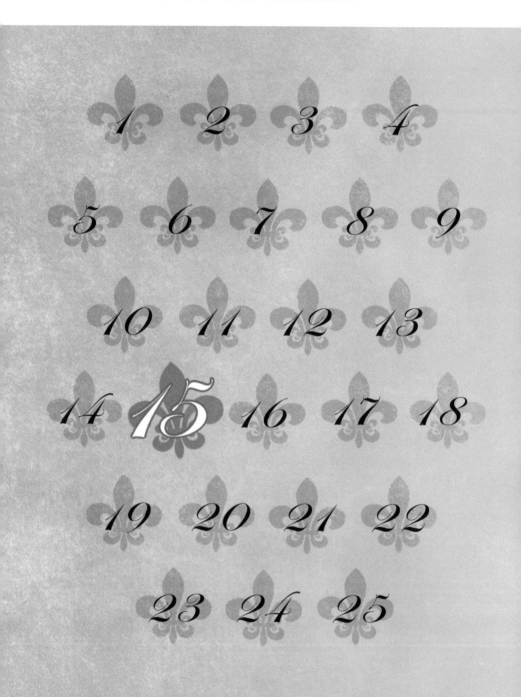

Day 15

TIP: Create drama and depth in your tree lighting.

Christmas Tree Lighting Pro Tip #3.

Before stringing lights on the tree, wrap a light set around the trunk first to add depth and sparkle to your tree. It takes some effort as you have to raise branches out of your way to wrap the light cord around the tree trunk, but it's worth the result.

Start at the top of the trunk with the non-plug end and work down to the bottom, plugging that set directly into your power strip.

This is one of the secrets to tree decoration that really made a difference in our tree lighting. It's simple and the depth it adds is noticeable.

One of my dearest clients appreciates detail
as much as I do. She used this tip of wrapping a light set
round the trunk first and when she completed putting all
lights on her tree, she told me she was astonished that such
a small detail could be so impactful!

Day 15 Organizing Concept

Organize Creatively

Day 16

TIP: Use 100 lights
per foot of tree.

CHRISTMAS TREE LIGHTING Pro Tip #4 is to use many more lights than you may be used to using. Hence the pro formula here.

We buy a 7-foot tall Fraser Fir, because it has strong branches for our heavy glass and ceramic ornaments. We use 1,000 mini multi-color lights.

Happy lighting!

Day 16 Organizing Concept

Organize Creatively

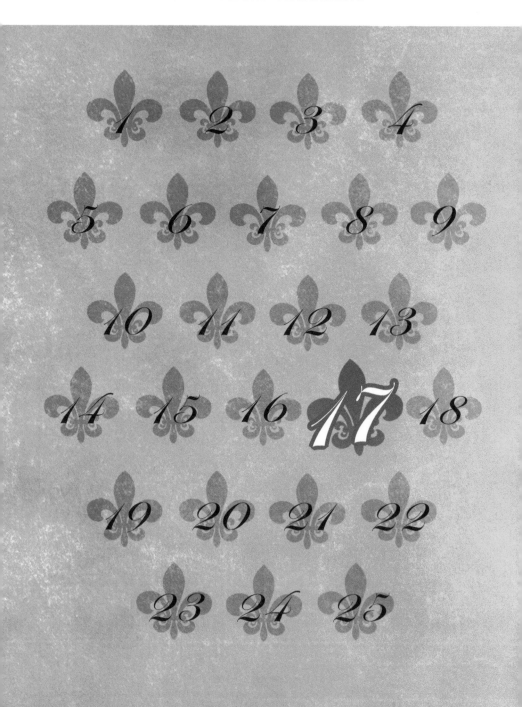

TIP: A new way to light your Christmas tree!

CHRISTMAS TREE LIGHTING Pro Tip #5 will revolutionize the way you look at lighting.

Instead of wrapping tree lights around the tree, divide the tree mentally into three sections. Start at the top and work your way down the tree. Weave the strings of lights up and down in a vertical wave within the section you are working on. Wrap the lights from trunk to branch tip every few large branches. You do not have to wrap each branch.

I don't know why we learn to wrap our Christmas lights all the way around the tree. It makes for harder work. A neighbor who is an engineer taught me this trick, and I have used it ever since. It's easier to stay in one section rather than going around the entire tree. It's also easier to pull the lights off when it's time to take down the tree.

Even if you didn't use this tip this year, remember it for next year. Honestly, once you try it, you never go back to the wrap around.

Lighting Your Christmas Tree

Divide your tree mentally into 3 sections.

Light one section at a time.

String lights up and down not around.

Day 17 Organizing Concept

Simplify & Clarify

Day 18

TIP: Start at the top of the tree with the non-plug end.

CHRISTMAS TREE LIGHTING Pro Tip #6.

Drop the non-plug end along the trunk securing the light strand by tying it around the trunk. Hide the non-plug end along the trunk or behind/under your tree topper ornament.

We hide ours under our St. Nicholas tree topper. Some people like a star or an angel on the top of their tree, but all our trees, even our mini ones, have a Santa.

Now, think back to Day 8 about how to store your Christmas tree lights in which I recommended writing down tree-lighting notes (such as these Christmas Tree Lighting Pro Tips) and storing it with your lights.

The first note I ever wrote in my tree-lighting notes was this tip of starting with the non-plug end before beginning to string our Christmas tree. Why? Because before I wrote down a reminder, I would start stringing and then realize I'd forgotten to start with the proper light strand end. By the time I remembered, I was halfway through!

DAY 18 Organizing Concept

Simplify & Clarify

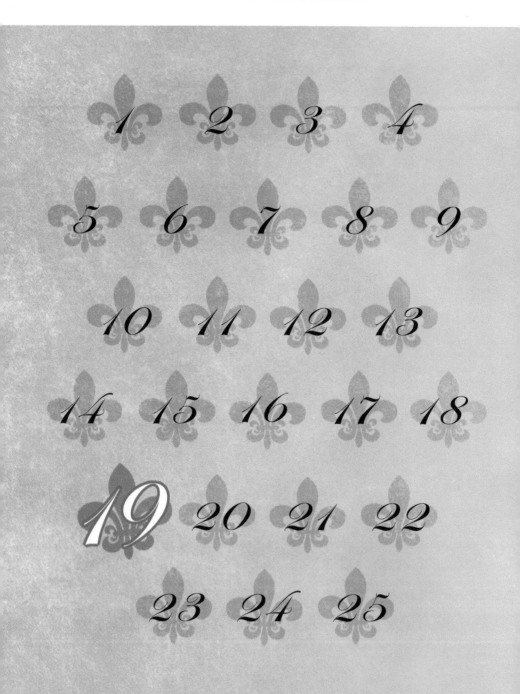

Day 19

TIP: Water your Christmas tree the simple way.

WATER SPOUTS ARE an invention that make my life—and many others'—so much easier. These are designed with a plastic green funnel that tapers into a long tube with a removable wooden dowel used as a water gauge. You hide the water spout against the trunk of your tree, inserting the tube into your tree stand. To check the water level, just insert the dowel into the funnel, removing it to add water. When you water your Christmas tree you pour the water into the funnel so it trickles directly into the tree stand. No more water mess and awkward refilling of the tree. No more bending down to check the tree water level.

Sometimes the simplest things can make all the difference. This spout isn't expensive, and it really does the job. I created a simple trick to fill my Christmas tree stand to the right level each time. I use a permanent marker to mark the level of the preferred water line on the dowel, so I know exactly when the water is filled near the top.

For more information and how to order this handy watering tool, search Christmas Tree-Watering Spout in your computer's browser.

Christmas Tree-Watering Spout

BONUS *Tip*

For spout refills use an old plastic half-gallon bottle or carton (like an apple juice bottle) and fill with tepid water. The bottle or carton opening fits well in the spout so no spills.

Day 19 Organizing Concept

Use Quality Supplies

Day 20

TIP: Ornament and decoration repair.

EVERY YEAR, SOME piece of decoration comes off an ornament. With a glue gun, the repair is instant.

Use a mini glue gun, like the one shown on page 115, for repairs.

http://bit.ly/Mini-GlueGun

A mini glue gun is a great item to pack with your ornaments. I have my mini glue gun and glue sticks at the ready every Christmas.

Not only that, because glue guns come in handy for so many tasks, they can make great gifts. I just gave a mini glue gun as a Christmas gift to a friend. She was jumping for joy!

Day 20 Organizing Concept

Prepare Ahead

TIP: Make your own kissing ball and spice it up!

WE LOVE HANGING our Christmas Kissing Balls from two large hooks above our front porch railing, visually ringing in the season as neighbors drive by. In case you aren't familiar with this tradition, a kissing ball is an evergreen (often live) ornamentation, made, not surprisingly, in the shape of a ball. Histor-ically they were hung from the ceiling in doorways or passageways to give bless-

ings to those who passed under them. No one passes under our kissing balls hung over our front porch railing, but it's a sweet

thought that blessings from them surround our house and are bestowed on all those who enter. Kissing balls are festive and their round shape reminds me of a large evergreen ornament. They add visual charm when hung from any ceiling or hook.

For years, I would buy two fresh kissing balls to hang on outside hooks on our front porch. But, through the years, their prices increased. Once I became a single mama, that cost in the name of décor became challenging … still, it was an important tradition for me.

Finally, I found artificial kissing balls that

were inexpensive, and I customized them with mini poinsettia flowers from a craft store. I added dangling Christmas red ribbons on a wooden skewer with my trusty glue gun. This year, I've added some artificial greens to make them fuller.

One of my clients asked me if my kissing balls are another version of the mistletoe tradition. To be honest, I wondered myself, but don't actually know. She suggested a new tradition—Kissing Ball Mistletoe—because the better coverage from above allows more chances of snagging a kiss.

Day 21 Organizing Concept

Organize Creatively

Day 22

S UCH AS *THE Elf on the Shelf*, cookies and milk for Santa, or reading *'Twas the Night Before Christmas.* A few of our Christmas traditions:

- ❧ Homemade Scottish shortbread
- ❧ Homemade Linzer tortes
- ❧ Jul's' Homemade Delectable Apple Pie
- ❧ Sending a yearly family photo Christmas card
- ❧ Santa atop our Christmas trees—*We put Saint Nicholas above our tree instead of a star or angel. Every tree of ours has a Santa on top, even our mini trees.*

✤ Reading *A Visit From Saint Nicholas* by Clement
Clarke Moore (commonly referred to as 'Twas the
Night Before Christmas)*

*My boys loved snuggling up to Mama as I read our special
Christmas story, *'Twas the Night Before Christmas*. We carried on this tradition from their Papa's family. The book is
easily available everywhere and even online.

Many people love *The Elf on the Shelf,* a recent tradition based on the book of the same name by Carol Aebersold and Chanda Bell. It involves taking a small stuffed toy Elf and placing it somewhere in the house. The idea for this is that the Elf is Santa's little helper. He watches the children in the house during the day, seeing if they behave or not, and then flies back each night to the North Pole to give Santa a report. There are two rules to the game: first, the children aren't allowed to touch the Elf or the Elf loses his or her magic; the second rule is that while the Elf will not "speak or move" while children are awake, it "disappears" at night and "reappears" in a different place in the house the next day. Now the kids have to figure out where the Elf has landed.

This new tradition encourages kids to behave and is popular in households with younger children, who love discovering where their Elf on the Shelf is each day. We've even seen grown kids have fun discovering where the house Elf is hidden!

Here are some of our past family photo Christmas cards.

One of my clients shared this story with me:

"Our family tradition when my two sons were young, was to read one or two children's Christmas books aloud every night from December 1st to 24th. The last would always be 'Twas the Night Before Christmas."

Another client, an Australian, says she wouldn't dream of not having turkey with brandy sauce, vegetables and "watching the Christmas carols," Aussie speak for watching Christmas shows on TV. (I may have to come over for Christmas!)

Day 22 Organizing Concept

Simplify & Clarify

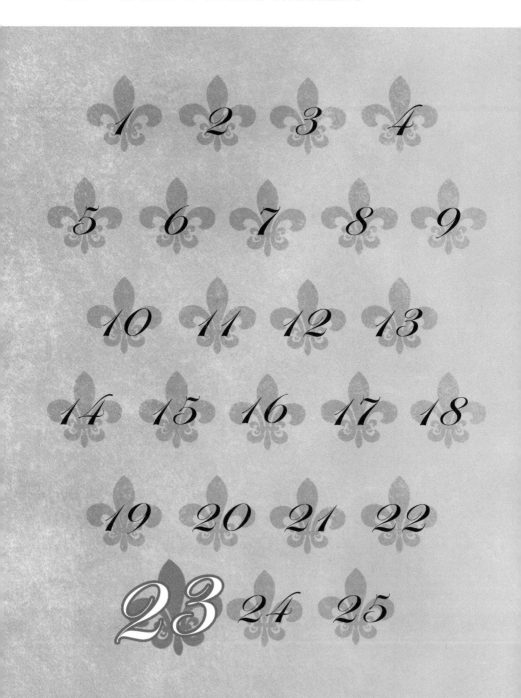

Day 23

TIP: Simplify addressing holiday cards.

CREATE A MASTER spreadsheet in Excel with separate fields for all this information:

First Name
Last Name
Address 1
Address 2
Town
State
Zip
Country (if necessary)

Next, create a Mail Merge in Word to print labels.

If you have beautiful penmanship and prefer to hand address each card, use the Excel master list as a checklist. One of our neighbors sends us a yearly Christmas card addressing our envelope with stylish calligraphy.

When I get ready to send out my 100 Christmas cards, I ready all my card supplies:

- ✤ Holiday Forever stamps
- ✤ Our return address labels
- ✤ My Mail Merge addressee labels
- ✤ Christmas stickers
- ✤ Our Christmas yearly letter
- ✤ Our Christmas card

I can quickly assemble all the cards while watching *It's a Wonderful Life* or *The Grinch Who Stole Christmas*, which reminds me of other traditions in our home.

One of my clients sent 450 cards each year at holiday time. I created an organized, alphabetized and easy-to-edit spreadsheet and *it proved invaluable.*

Day 23 Organizing Concept

Simplify & Clarify

Day 24

TIP: Label boxes by room for storage.

ERE'S A SECRET organizing tip that I can't wait to share with you. Store your boxes labeled by the room the decorations will be displayed; this way you can easily take the boxes into the appropriate room to decorate. After the holidays just pack each room up into its own labeled boxes.

We have many, many Christmas decorations. It's the one area where I unleash the collector in me. I decorate so many of the rooms in our house and it's a special time for us.

There's my Santa Mantle. And yes, the boys get me a special Santa from around the world every year. We have our Department 56 Snowbabies, our Christmas snow globes, elf pull-string ornaments and wooden Christmas train puzzles.

Each and every one of these ornaments gives me joy! I honor them by storing them in boxes that keep them preserved year after year.

Foyer Christmas
decorations,
labeled

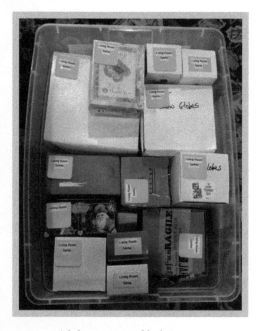

Living room Christmas
Santas, labeled

I color-coordinate labels for the different rooms. Then I store those boxes or plastic zipper bags in 18-gallon plastic totes.

Even if I have to mix a plastic tote with some boxes from the living room and some boxes from the dining room, the color labels make it instantly identifiable.

Decorated living room fireplace: Santa Mantle

Dining room Christmas decorations, labeled

Mudroom Christmas decorations, labeled

Day 24 Organizing Concept

Simplify & Clarify

Happy Christmas! Enjoy The Fun!

No ORGANIZING TODAY. These are the important things:

Family ~ Friends ~ Laughter ~ Love!

And enjoy my video!

 https://youtu.be/WSvBØFMk5VQ

Day 25 Organizing Concept

Keep It Fun!

BOXING DAY
Bonus

julsarthur.com

Day 26

BONUS!

I ASKED MY CLAN: "What holiday stress is challenging you right now?"

Number one answer? Figuring out unique gifts for everyone.

I want to offer some top-of-mind ideas.

I was feeling this challenge recently when I asked my sons, Tyryn and Skylyr, what they wanted for Christmas. Both independently replied, "Nothing."

I am happy I raised children who are not materialistic and value more than just things. However, I don't want to put "nothing" under the Christmas tree. Besides, isn't it great to get a gift we might not think to get for ourselves?

Step 1:

Make a list of what comes to mind about the person … his or her interests.

Mayhap he or she loves zombie books or mysteries. Brainstorm things this person enjoys—activities, experiences, or things. Does the person love yoga? Maybe a few prepaid sessions to yoga class would be great. Me? I like facials or having my nails done, so gift certificates from my boys to my favorite salon work great. My elder son is an amazing puzzler. Last year I got him a 3D puzzle.

Step 2:

Create a gift basket or care package of several smaller gifts.

How about a gift basket or care package with the person's favorite goodies? Always useful items? For example, this year for my sons, it was car chargers for their phones. Hope that starts you off!

Step 3:

Gift an experience rather than a thing.

This could even include a homemade coupon book* filled with thoughtful coupons such as:

- ✤ Dinner and a movie
- ✤ Back massage
- ✤ Foot massage
- ✤ No-chore freebie day

*When my sons were little, I gave them homemade coupons for staying up an extra half hour or special time with Mama. They loved those gifts possibly more than their Legos!

RECIPE
Bonus

julsarthur.com

Day 27

BONUS!

WHEN YOU GET invited to a lot of holiday parties, you need something easy to make and take.

This is one of my favorite recipes to bring to someone's house, or for our own party, as it's so easy to make and can be made the day before. Plus, you can keep the ingredients on hand to whip up when wanted.

I always keep extra butter and cream cheese in the fridge, and packages of frozen chopped spinach in the freezer. And I have breadcrumbs and spices in the spice cabinet and pantry at all times.

I love to make this recipe the day before and take it along in a foil pie plate so I don't have to worry about retrieving my dish.

RECIPE: Spinach Pie
From the kitchen of Jul's

INGREDIENTS

2 10-oz pkgs frozen spinach–cooked, drained

1 8-oz pkg cream cheese

1/2 stick butter, cut into two halves

1/4 teaspoon garlic powder

Salt & black pepper to taste

3/4 cup plain bread crumbs

3/4 teaspoon rubbed sage

DIRECTIONS

Microwave spinach about 15 min on high, drain.

Melt 1/4 stick butter, mix with bread crumbs.

Pour plain bread crumbs into a small bowl and mix in rubbed sage, set aside for topping.

Put the drained spinach into a saucepan on medium low heat, add: cream cheese, 1/4 stick butter, salt, pepper and garlic powder stirring to combine. Pour creamy spinach mixture into a 9-inch pie pan. Top with bread crumb mix.

Preheat oven to 350°. Bake 30 min, until golden brown.
Can be made day before and reheated.

I hope you enjoyed these 25 Days of Holiday Organizing!

Here's the thing. I want you to implement at least one of these 25 organizing tips into your life. You'll be amazed at the domino effect it will have on making you feel more on top of your holiday decorations.

Don't stop there...

Get your **completely FREE** consultation call!
A 20-minute 1:1 call with me, Jul's,
to help you start on your holiday organizing tasks...
or, perhaps, your personal organizing path.

Go to:

 http://bit.ly/JulsClarityCall

Happy holidays! Happy organizing!

Jul's xox

Let's Connect

I'D LOVE TO **hear from you! Share Your Wins with Me** on my Facebook page to get answers and more inspiration.

Leave me a comment on Facebook: https://www.facebook.com/JulsArthurOrganizing/

- ⚜ About how organizing something in your home or life has added to your sense of calm.

- ⚜ Share some of the "homes" you've created for your holiday items that work for you and your family. For example, a special drawer or CD box for storing your holiday music or how you keep your holiday recipes easily available.

- ⚜ What are some ways your parents helped you to get organized for the holidays? Have you handed these down to your children?

- ⚜ I'm a traditional lass. I love Christmas traditions. What are your holiday traditions?

For more information about personal organizing and Jul's, visit my website—https://julsarthur.com

About the Author

*J*UL'S ARTHUR is a professional organizer and daily money manager. She works with individuals and companies in-person and virtually all over the world to help them find organizational harmony at home and in the office.

Her clients include discerning professionals, busy moms, their families and seniors. Always a holiday enthusiast, Jul's has helped many people with holiday organizing, inspiration and decoration. Her specialties include paper taming, managing bills, home and office-filing systems, decluttering, photo organizing and home or office moves. The calm, supportive approach Jul's uses always guides her clients to the successful outcome they envision.

This is her first book. Her goal is to provide readers with an interactive experience that is informative, accessible and engaging. Jul's believes in holidays infused with beauty, magic, fun, family, love and ease.

Lightning Source UK Ltd.
Milton Keynes UK
UKHW050710200521
384044UK00007B/82